DEVIL RAYS

DYNAMIC DANCERS

KATIE
LAJINESS

AWESOME ANIMAL
POWERS

Big Buddy Books
An Imprint of Abdo Publishing
abdopublishing.com

abdopublishing.com

Published by Abdo Publishing, a division of ABDO, PO Box 398166, Minneapolis, Minnesota 55439.
Copyright © 2019 by Abdo Consulting Group, Inc. International copyrights reserved in all countries.
No part of this book may be reproduced in any form without written permission from the publisher.
Big Buddy Books™ is a trademark and logo of Abdo Publishing.

Printed in the United States of America, North Mankato, Minnesota.
052018
092018

THIS BOOK CONTAINS
RECYCLED MATERIALS

Cover Photo: Wolfgang Pölzer/Alamy Stock Photo.
Interior Photos: Ben Horton/Getty Images (p. 17); imageBROKER/Alamy Stock Photo (pp. 15,
    27); Karen Debler/Alamy Stock Photo (p. 21); massimillano finzi/Alamy Stock Photo (p. 25);
    renacal1/Getty Images (p. 11); WaterFrame/Alamy Stock Photo (p. 7); Westend61/Getty
    Images (p. 29); wildestanimal/Getty Images (pp. 9, 23); Wolfgang Pölzer/Alamy Stock Photo
    (pp. 5, 19, 30).

Coordinating Series Editor: Tamara L. Britton
Contributing Editor: Jill Roesler
Graphic Design: Jenny Christensen, Erika Weldon

Library of Congress Control Number: 2017961386

Publisher's Cataloging-in-Publication Data

Names: Lajiness, Katie, author.
Title: Devil Rays: Dynamic dancers / by Katie Lajiness.
Other titles: Dynamic dancers
Description: Minneapolis, Minnesota : Abdo Publishing, 2019. | Series: Awesome animal
    powers | Includes online resources and index.
Identifiers: ISBN 9781532114984 (lib.bdg.) | ISBN 9781532155703 (ebook)
Subjects: LCSH: Marine fishes--Juvenile literature. | Rays (Fishes)--Juvenile literature. |
    Fishes--Behavior--Juvenile literature.
Classification: DDC 597.35--dc23

CONTENTS

THE DEVIL RAY

The world is full of awesome, powerful animals. Devil rays (dev-ihl RAYS) are amazing, dancing fish. Their uncommon body shapes allow them to be graceful swimmers. Despite their names, devil rays are not mean. In fact, they are very gentle.

DID YOU KNOW?

Some people confuse devil rays and manta rays. However, the two look different.

While feeding, devil rays can dive more than one mile (2 km) deep. And, they can stay underwater for up to 90 minutes.

BOLD BODIES

Devil rays have amazing bodies. They do not have bones! Instead, their bodies are made of **cartilage**. Devil rays' bodies are flat. And they are wider than they are long.

A devil ray's mouth extends across the front of its head. And it has two fins on either side of its mouth called **cephalic** fins.

DID YOU KNOW?

Devil rays can be reddish to olive brown in color. But they can also be bluish-gray or completely black.

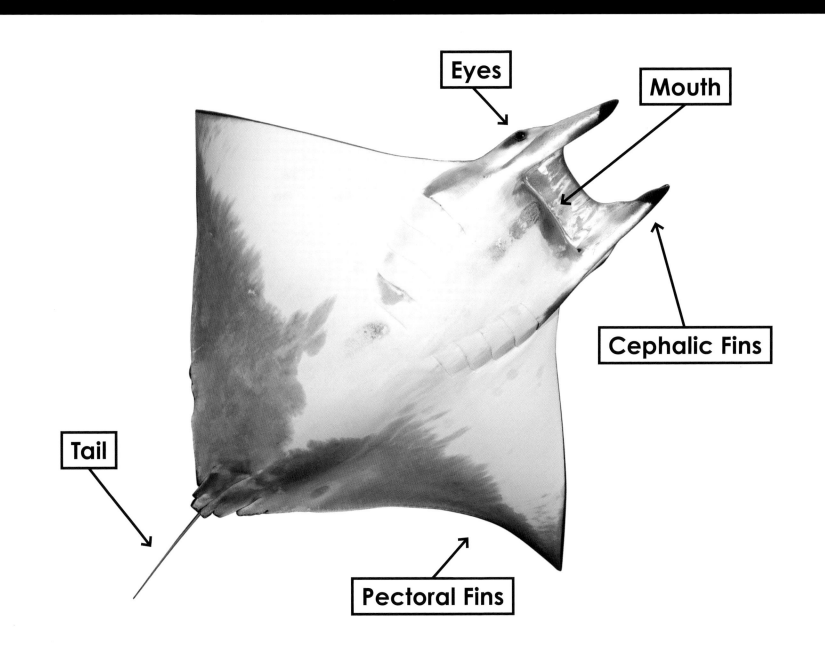

THAT'S AWESOME!

These fish look lively when they swim. Their fins move together in a smooth motion. Their large fins flap like underwater wings. Fins help devil rays swim fast and turn quickly.

Devil rays have been around for about 25 million years.

Devil rays often leap out of the water. Some believe they jump to **communicate** or to attract partners. Others think devil rays jump to remove **parasites** from their skin.

DID YOU KNOW?

Always moving, devil rays glide through the water even while they sleep!

These dancing fish can jump nearly seven feet (2 m) in the air!

WHERE IN THE

Devil rays mostly live in warm waters. They are found in the Mediterranean and Black seas, and near the North Atlantic Ocean. Some rays stay close to shore. But others like to swim in deeper parts of the ocean.

WORLD?

= WHERE DEVIL RAYS LIVE

ARCTIC
OCEAN

North
America

Europe

Asia

PACIFIC
OCEAN

NORTH
ATLANTIC
OCEAN

Africa

South
America

PACIFIC
OCEAN

INDIAN
OCEAN

Australia

SOUTH
ATLANTIC
OCEAN

N
W E
S

DAILY LIFE

Devil rays like to stay busy. They dive deep to hunt for food. Only three other types of fish dive as deep as devil rays. The rays swim about 13 miles (20 km) per hour on their way down.

Devil rays are related to sharks.

Before devil rays dive deep into the ocean, they must warm their bodies. So they swim near the surface of the water to heat themselves.

Then they dive deep into cold waters. They need to stay warm during a dive to maintain brain and eye function.

Rays only dive deep during the day. That is when the rays' food is easiest to find.

A DEVIL RAY'S LIFE

Tiny animals called remoras (rih-MOHR-uhs) clean devil rays' bodies. They cling on using their round sucker mouths.

The remoras remove small **parasites** from the rays' skin. In return, the rays protect the remoras from **predators**.

There are nine different species of devil ray. They all belong to the *mobula* family.

Every year, devil rays **migrate** to areas with more food. They follow their food source to warmer waters. Devil rays migrate up to 2,300 miles (3,800 km) over seven months.

As devil rays swim, they soar out of the water. When they land, it sounds like raindrops.

FAVORITE FOODS

Devil rays eat some of the smallest animals in the sea. These rays have no teeth. But they do have fins on either side of their mouths. These **cephalic** fins furl together to make a funnel when they swim. The fins funnel food directly into the rays' mouths!

The devil ray got its name because the cephalic fins look like devil horns!

BIRTH

Male devil rays must work hard to **mate** with a female. They chase the female all through the water. Then she selects one male with which to mate.

After mating, an egg hatches inside the female devil ray. She then gives birth to one pup.

A baby devil ray is called a pup. At birth, a pup is about 45 inches (1 m) wide and weighs about 25 pounds (11 kg).

DEVELOPMENT

A female devil ray begins **breeding** between ten and 15 years old. The female can be **pregnant** for up to two years!

A mother has a pup every two to five years. Once the pup is born, it immediately begins taking care of itself.

Devil rays can live
40 to 50 years.

FUTURE

Today, devil rays are in danger. Too many are fished out of the oceans. However, devil rays are not caught for their meat. Instead, parts of their bodies are used for **medicine**.

But this practice upsets many people. So today, **conservation** groups work hard to keep devil rays safe.

Devil rays produce few pups.
So, it is difficult for these animals
to build up their numbers.

FAST FACTS

ANIMAL TYPE: Fish

SIZE: 16 ft (5 m)

WEIGHT: 2,000 pounds (907 kg)

HABITAT: The North Atlantic Ocean, and the Mediterranean and Black seas

DIET: Small fish

AWESOME ANIMAL POWER: Devil rays swim gracefully through the ocean and leap high into the air.

GLOSSARY

breed to produce animals by mating.

cartilage (KAHR-tuh-lihj) matter that is tough and bendable. Cartilage is in a person's nose and ears.

cephalic (suh-FA-lihk) situated on, in, or near the head.

communicate (kuh-MYOO-nuh-kayt) to give and receive information, such as knowledge or news.

conservation (kahn-suhr-VAY-shuhn) work done to save land, water, and other natural resources.

mate to join as a couple in order to reproduce, or have babies.

medicine (MEH-duh-suhn) an item used in or on the body to treat an illness, ease pain, or heal a wound.

migrate to move from one place to another to find food or have babies.

parasite (PEHR-uh-site) a living thing that lives in or on another living thing. It gains from its host, which it usually hurts.

predator a person or animal that hunts and kills animals for food.

pregnant having one or more babies growing within the body.

ONLINE
RESOURCES

Booklinks
NONFICTION NETWORK
FREE! ONLINE NONFICTION RESOURCES

To learn more about devil rays, visit **abdobooklinks.com**. These links are routinely monitored and updated to provide the most current information available.

INDEX